HOW & WHY?

BIRDS USE THEIR BEAKS

Elaine Pascoe is the author of more than 20 acclaimed children's books on a wide range of subjects.
Dwight Kuhn's scientific expertise and artful eye work together with the camera to capture the awesome wonder of the natural world.

Please visit our web site at: www.garethstevens.com
For a free color catalog describing Gareth Stevens Publishing's list of high-quality books
and multimedia programs, call 1-800-542-2595 or fax your request to (414) 332-3567.

Library of Congress Cataloging-in-Publication Data

Pascoe, Elaine.
   Birds use their beaks / by Elaine Pascoe; photographs by Dwight Kuhn. — North American ed.
      p. cm. — (How & why: a springboards into science series)
   Includes bibliographical references and index.
   Summary: Explains how different kinds of birds use their beaks for such things as eating, preening,
and courtship displays.
   ISBN 0-8368-3008-3 (lib. bdg.)
   1. Bill (Anatomy)—Juvenile literature. [1. Bill (Anatomy). 2. Birds.] I. Kuhn, Dwight, ill. II. Title.
QL697.P37   2002
598.14—dc21   2001049496

This North American edition first published in 2002 by
Gareth Stevens Publishing
A World Almanac Education Group Company
330 West Olive Street, Suite 100
Milwaukee, WI 53212 USA

First published in the United States in 2000 by Creative Teaching Press, Inc., P.O. Box 2723, Huntington Beach, CA 92647-0723.
Text © 2000 by Elaine Pascoe; photographs © 2000 by Dwight Kuhn. Additional end matter © 2002 by Gareth Stevens, Inc.

Gareth Stevens editor: Mary Dykstra
Gareth Stevens designer: Tammy Gruenewald

Printed in the United States of America

1 2 3 4 5 6 7 8 9 06 05 04 03 02

HOW & WHY ?

BIRDS USE THEIR BEAKS

by Elaine Pascoe
photographs by Dwight Kuhn

A SPRINGBOARDS INTO SCIENCE SERIES

Gareth Stevens Publishing
A WORLD ALMANAC EDUCATION GROUP COMPANY

When an Arctic tern sees danger, it opens its beak wide and calls out a warning.

A sparrow opens its beak to sing a song.

A bird's beak, or bill, is its mouth, but it is also a wonderful tool. Birds use their tough, hard beaks to grab and eat food, to carry things, to build their nests, to clean their feathers, and to do many other jobs.

In a pond, a mallard duck dips its bill into the water as it swims along. The duck is looking for the tiny water plants and insects it likes to eat.

The duck's wide, flat bill acts like a strainer, collecting food from the water. This way of getting food is called dabbling.

The beaks of many birds are specially shaped to help the birds eat certain foods. A parrot's hooked beak is a powerful seed cracker. The beak's sharp edges can break open even the toughest seed coverings.

A hummingbird has a long, slender beak. This shape is perfect for reaching deep into the center of a flower to drink the nectar there. Nectar is a hummingbird's favorite food.

Birds use their beaks to bring food to their young, too. A robin catches a worm with its beak and carries the worm back to its nest, where hungry babies are waiting for a meal. Baby birds open their beaks wide to get the food.

An Atlantic puffin goes fishing for its family. It catches one fish after another, holding all the fish in its bill. A puffin can carry up to thirty fish at a time! And a puffin can even open its bill without dropping the fish. It uses its tongue to hold the fish against spines in the roof of its mouth.

A puffin's big bill has another special purpose. Its bright colors help the bird attract a mate.

When male puffins go courting, they bob their heads up and down. They seem to be showing off their colorful bills. Male and female puffins get to know each other by rubbing their bills against each other's.

13

Beaks are great tools for building nests. This cedar waxwing found a piece of thread that is just right for its nest. It holds the thread in its beak to carry the thread to its nesting site.

A yellow warbler uses its beak to weave plant fibers into its nest. These fibers make a soft resting place for the bird's eggs.

Birds use their beaks for all kinds of jobs. If a tern's egg rolls out of its nest, the tern pushes the egg back into the nest with its beak.

A brown pelican uses its huge bill to preen, or comb, its feathers. All birds preen their feathers this way. Preening is very important. It cleans the feathers and spreads oil over them to keep them waterproof.

Can you answer these "HOW & WHY" questions?

1. Why does a mallard duck dip its bill in water?

2. How does a hummingbird get nectar?

3. How can an Atlantic puffin carry so many fish at once?

4. How does a male puffin court a mate?

5. How does a yellow warbler use its beak when it is building a nest?

6. Why is preening important for birds?

(See page 20 for answers.)

ANSWERS

1. A mallard duck uses its bill as a strainer to get food out of the water.

2. A hummingbird pushes its long, slender beak deep into the center of a flower and sips out the flower's nectar.

3. A puffin has spines on the roof of its mouth to help the bird hold the fish it is carrying without dropping them.

4. First, a male puffin bobs its head up and down, showing off its bill, to attract a mate. After a male attracts a female, the two puffins rub their large bills together to get to know each other.

5. A yellow warbler uses its beak to weave soft plant fibers into its nest.

6. Birds preen, or comb, their feathers to keep them clean and to spread oil over the feathers to keep them waterproof.

Beak and Bath

Birds use their beaks to preen, keeping their feathers clean and in good condition. You can help birds preen by putting a birdbath in your backyard and keeping it filled with water. Many stores sell birdbaths, but you can make one of your own using a garbage can cover or some other wide, shallow pan. If the inside surface of the pan is slippery, put a layer of small stones on the bottom of it to give the birds better footing. Put your birdbath near some bushes or trees, so the birds will have a safe shelter nearby, then fill up the "tub!"

From Head to Toe

Just as birds' beaks are different sizes and shapes for special purposes, their feet are different, too. Fold a piece of paper in half the long way. On one side of the paper, draw pictures of different kinds of beaks, such as the wide bill of a duck or the sharp, curved beak of a hawk or an eagle. On the other side of the paper, draw a picture of that bird's feet. For example, across from the hawk's beak you would draw feet with sharp talons for catching prey. Use books or the Internet to make sure each bird is drawn correctly from head to toe.

Getting the Point

Put some raisins into a bowl to try a simple experiment. First, try to spear a raisin and remove it from the bowl using a straw. Then try again with a toothpick. Which worked better? Why? Find pictures of birds with beaks that are good for spearing. What kinds of foods do these birds eat?

GLOSSARY

attract: to draw someone or something closer by causing excitement or interest.

courting: behaving in a special way to attract a mate.

dabbling: reaching with a beak, or bill, into shallow water to get food.

fibers: threadlike strands of a natural or manmade material.

mate (n): either the male or female in a pair of animals that join to produce young.

nectar: the sweet liquid in flowers that many insects and birds like to drink.

pond: a body of water smaller than a lake.

preen: to clean or smooth feathers with a beak, or bill.

seed coverings: the protective coatings or shells that cover seeds.

site: the place where a structure was or will be built, or where an activity or event has occurred or will occur.

slender: thin and often tall or long.

spines: the stiff, sharp, needlelike parts that stick out of an animal or a plant.

strainer: a tool often found in the kitchen that separates solids from liquids by holding back the solids but letting the liquids pass through.

tern: a small seabird that is a member of the gull family.

warbler: a small, brightly colored songbird.

waterproof: able to keep water from passing through.

weave: to pass threads or thin strips over and under each other to hold them in place.

More Books to Read

The Beak Book. Pamela Chanko (Scholastic)
Beaks and Noses. Head to Tail (series). Theresa Greenaway (Raintree/Steck-Vaughn)
Birds. Wonderful World of Animals (series). Beatrice MacLeod (Gareth Stevens)
Flying Brown Pelicans. Anne Welsbacher (Lerner)
Talons, Beaks, and Jaws. Animal Weapons (series). Lynn M. Stone (Rourke Press)
Unbeatable Beaks. Stephen R. Swinburne (Henry Holt & Company)

Videos

All About Animals: Feathered Friends. (National Geographic)
Amazing Animals: Birds of Prey. (DK Vision)
Of Birds, Beaks, and Behavior. (Coronet)

Web Sites

www.earthlife.net/birds/bills.html
www.enchantedlearning.com/crafts/Birdcard.shtml
www.fonz.org/education/sciandtech/birds/birdsv4frame.htm

Some web sites stay current longer than others. For additional web sites, use a good search engine to locate the following topics: *beaks, bills, bird anatomy, birds,* and *preening.*

INDEX